How to use this book

Follow the advice, in italics, given for you on each page.
Support the children as they read the text that is shaded in cream.
***Praise** the children at every step!*

Detailed guidance is provided in the Read Write Inc. Phonics Handbook.

8 reading activities

Children:
- *Practise reading the speed sounds.*
- *Read the green, red and challenge words for the story.*
- *Listen as you read the introduction.*
- *Discuss the vocabulary check with you.*
- *Read the story.*
- *Re-read the story and discuss the 'questions to talk about'.*
- *Re-read the story with fluency and expression.*
- *Practise reading the speed words.*

Speed sounds

Consonants *Say the pure sounds (do not add 'uh').*

f ff	l ll	m	n	r	s ss	v ve	z zz s	sh	(th)	ng nk

b bb	c k (ck)	d	g gg	h	j	p	qu	t	w wh	x	y	ch tch

Vowels *Say the vowel sound and then the word, e.g. 'a', 'at'.*

at	hen	in	on	up	day	see	high	blow	zoo

Each box contains one sound but sometimes more than one grapheme. Focus graphemes are **circled**.

Green words

Read in Fred Talk (pure sounds).

hop   at   wi<u>th</u>   and   spot   on   run

skip   ba<u>ck</u>   bend   ki<u>ck</u>   flop

Red words

<u>the</u>   do

Vocabulary check

Discuss the meaning (as used in the story) after the children have read the word.

definition:

back flip   a backward somersault in the air

hand stand   standing on your hands instead of your feet

Punctuation to note in this story:

Hop Skip Bend	Capital letters that start sentences
.	Full stop at the end of each sentence
!	Exclamation mark used to show surprise
...	Wait and see

The get fit club

Introduction

Do you like doing activities to keep fit? What do you do to keep fit? You can do lots of activities: running, swimming, gymnastics or even football to get fit.

The people in this story have all joined a get fit club.

They have fun doing lots of exercises like hopping, running, hand stands and back flips! How do they feel after all this activity? Let's find out.

Story written by Cynthia Rider
Illustrated by Tim Archbold

Hop with us at the get fit club.
Hop, hop, hop, and …

run on the spot.

Skip with us
at the get fit club.

Skip, skip, skip, and
do a back flip.

Bend with us
at the get fit club.

Bend, bend, bend, and
do a hand stand.

Flop with us
at the get fit club.

Flop!

Flop!

Flop!

Questions to talk about

FIND IT QUESTIONS
✓ Turn to the page
✓ Read the question to the children
✓ Find the answer

Page 8-9:   What exercise came after hopping?

Page 11:   What exercise came before the hand stand?

Page 12-13:   Why do the people flop at the end of the story?